Just ADD *Color*

KALEIDOSCOPES

BARRON'S

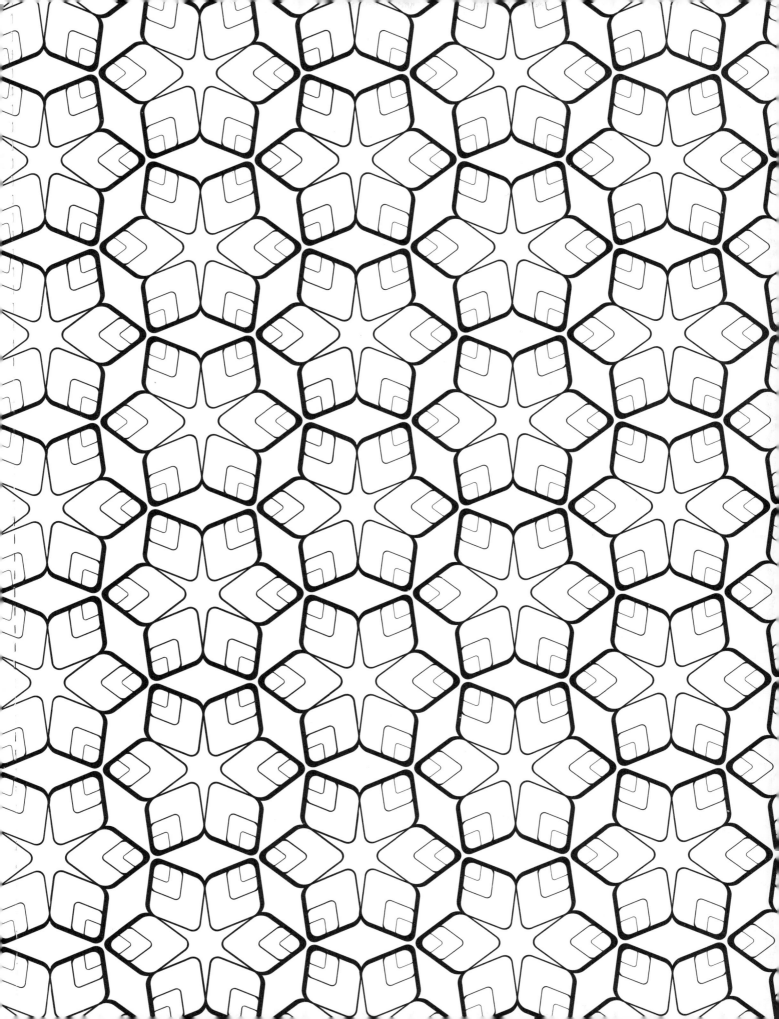

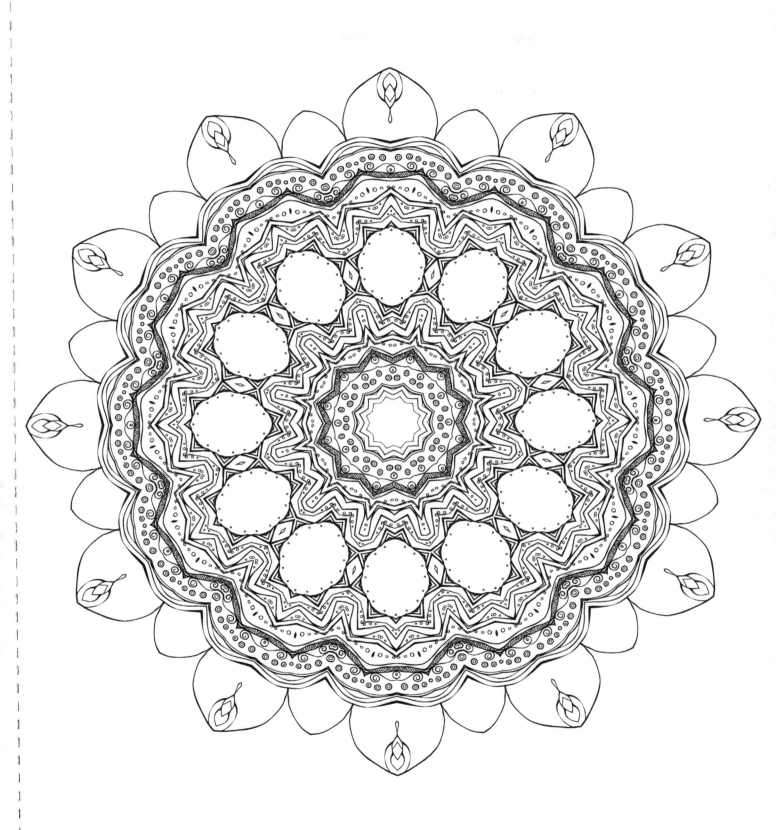

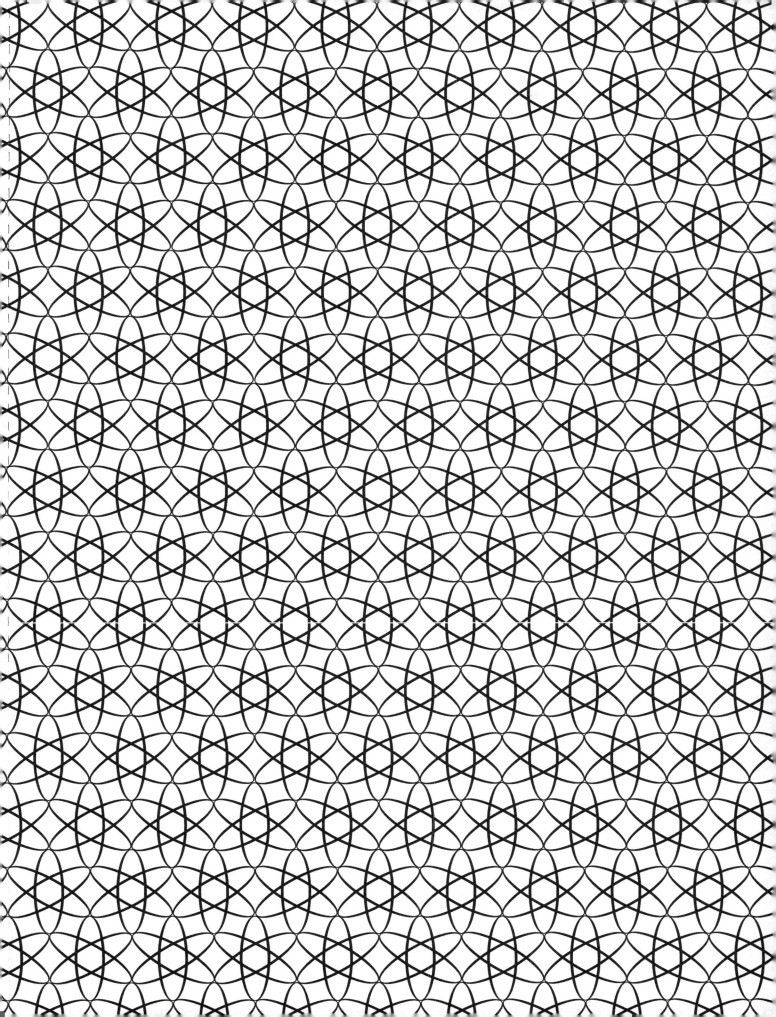

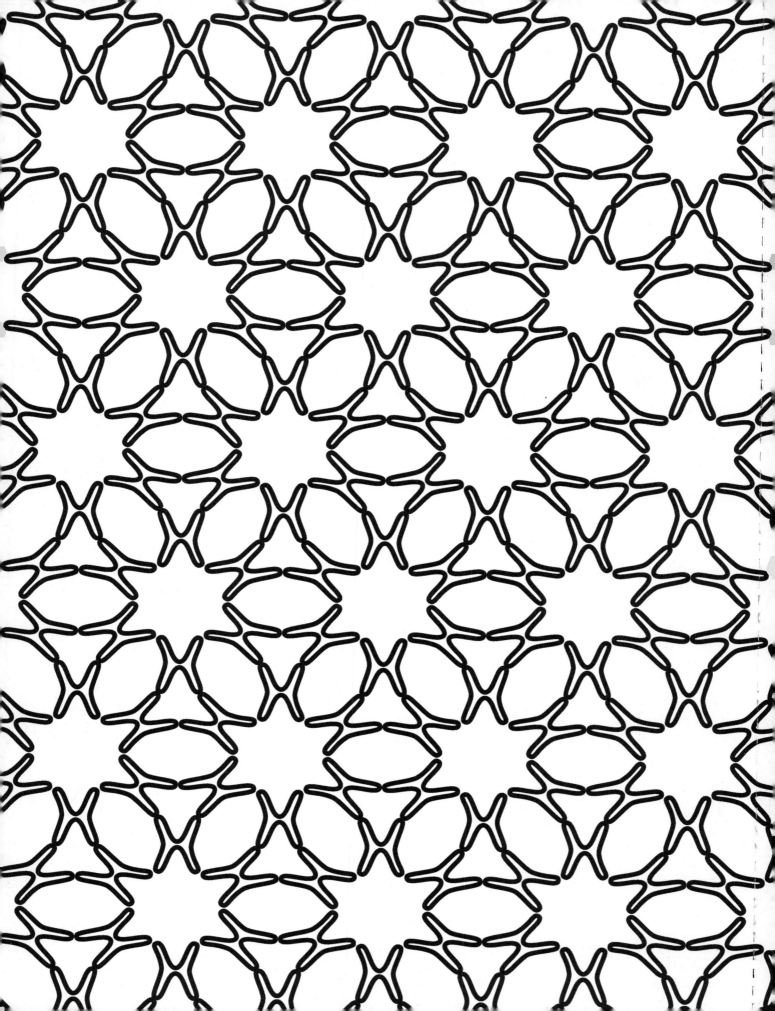

First edition for North America published in 2015 by Barron's Educational Series, Inc.

© Copyright 2015 by Carlton Publishing Group.

No part of this publication may be reproduced or distributed in any form or by any means without the written permission of the copyright owner.

All inquiries should be addressed to:

Barron's Educational Series, Inc.
250 Wireless Boulevard
Hauppauge, New York 11788

www.barronseduc.com

ISBN: 978-1-4380-0761-8

Manufactured by: RR Donnelley Asia, Dongguan, China

Printed in China

9 8 7 6 5 4 3 2